All Kinds of Plants

Carrie Branigan
and Richard Dunne

A⁺

Smart Apple Media

First published in 2004 by Franklin Watts
96 Leonard Street, London EC2A 4XD

Franklin Watts Australia
45–51 Huntley Street, Alexandria NSW 2015

Editor: Kate Newport, Art director: Jonathan Hair, Designer: Michael Leaman
Design Partnership, Line illustrator: Jeremy Leaman, Consultant: Gill Matthews,
nonfiction literacy consultant and Inset trainer

Picture credits:
Peter Arnold/Still Pictures: 14. Frank Blackburn/Ecoscene: 9t.
Nigel Cattlin/Holt Studios: front cover top, 6r, 9b, 15t, 17t,
17b, 18bl, 18cr, 19cl, 19cl, 19cr. Anthony Cooper/Ecoscene: 18cl. Corbis: 23c. Stephen Coyne/Ecoscene: 23t.
Alan & Linda Detrick/Holt Studios: 7l, 7r. Ric Ergenbright/Corbis: 22b.
Garden World Images: 20br. Bob Gibbons/Holt Studios: 10.
Chinch Gryniewicz/Ecoscene: 13, 21c. Angela Hampton/Ecoscene: 26.
Wayne Lawler/Ecoscene: 27. Andrew Linscott/Holt Studios: 20cl.
Rosie Mayer/Holt Studios: 23cl. Sally Morgan/Ecoscene: 6l, 11.
Tony Page/Ecoscene: front cover below. Primrose Peacock/Holt Studios: 12t. Promeck Services/Ecoscene: 16t.
Norman Rout/Ecoscene: 8. Paul Thompson/Ecoscene: 22c.
Francesco Venturi/Corbis: 25b. Douglas P. Wilson/FLPA/Corbis: 12b.
Picture research: Diana Morris.
All other photography by Ray Moller.

Published in the United States by Smart Apple Media
2140 Howard Drive West, North Mankato, Minnesota 56003

Library of Congress Cataloging-in-Publication Data

Branigan, Carrie.
All kinds of plants / by Carrie Branigan and Richard Dunne.
p. cm. — (World of plants)
ISBN 1-58340-610-7
1. Botany—Juvenile literature. 2. Plants—Juvenile literature
I. Dunne, Richard. II. Title. III. Series.

QK49.B73 2005
580—dc22   2004059965

2 4 6 8 9 7 5 3 1

Contents

All Kinds of Plants

There are many different plants. They grow in different shapes and sizes. They grow all around the world.

Some plants are very large.

Some plants are very small.

▲ The buttercup is a small yellow **flower** that grows in Europe.

▲ The giant redwood is a very large tree that grows in the United States.

Some plants are very tall.

◀ Bamboo is a tall grass that grows in Asia.

Some plants are very prickly.

▼ The cactus is a prickly plant that grows in deserts.

Can you find any large, small, tall, or prickly plants near where you live?

Plants with Flowers

Many plants grow flowers.
They are called flowering plants.

▲ A fruit tree grows many flowers in the spring. They are called **blossoms**.

flower

petal

stem

leaf

Some plants grow just one flower.

A poppy has red **petals**.

Seeds are made in flowers.

New poppy plants grow from poppy seeds.

Go for a walk in the spring or summer. How many different flowers can you see? What colors are the petals?

Plants with Cones

Some plants have **cones** instead of flowers. Seeds are made inside the cones.

Cones grow on trees called conifers.

◄ This conifer is a pine tree.

Pine trees grow in cold places where there is often snow. They grow lots of cones.

Cones have scales. They protect the seeds.

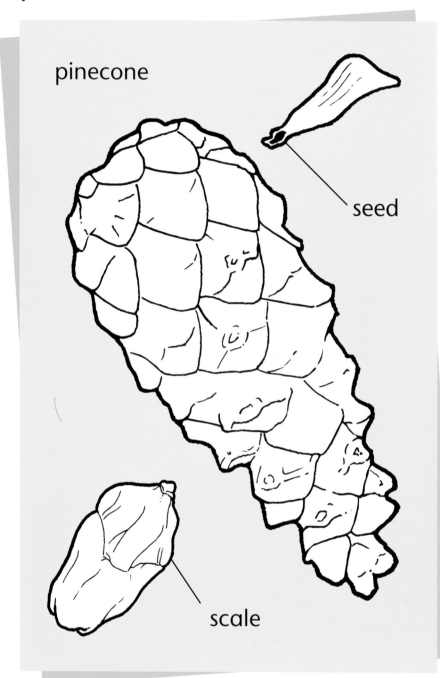

pinecone

seed

scale

New pine trees grow from a seed.

▲ A pine-cone

Conifers grow where it snows. How do you think their hard, pointy cones help to protect the seeds from the snow?

Plants without Flowers or Cones

Some plants do not grow flowers or cones.

◀ Bladder wrack is a seaweed. Air bubbles in its **fronds** help the plant float in water.

Seaweed and ferns grow **spores**. The spores form on the plants' fronds, which are like **leaves**.

Ferns usually grow in woods. A fern makes thousands of tiny spores under its fronds.

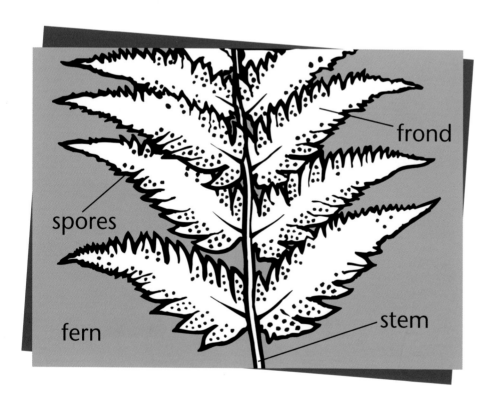

frond

spores

fern

stem

New ferns grow from the spores.

Next time you walk on the beach or in the woods, look for seaweeds or ferns.

Food Makers

Plants need food to stay alive, just like us. But they don't eat food. They make it inside their leaves.

Most plants have green leaves.

◀ A cabbage makes its food in its green leaves.

Leaves contain green coloring called **chlorophyll**. Chlorophyll works with water, air, and sunlight to make the plant's food.

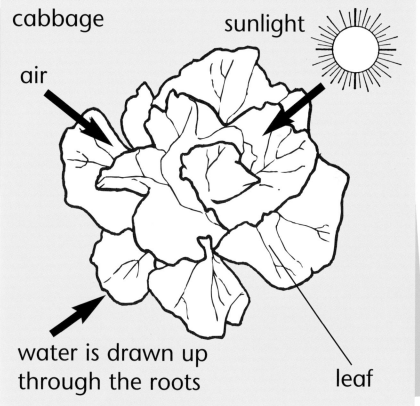

cabbage

air

sunlight

water is drawn up through the roots

leaf

Take a walk outside. Look at the leaves of different plants. How many of them are green?

Plants as Food

Plants are very important because animals and people need them as food.

▲ Cows eat grass.

▲ **Fruits, vegetables**, bread, pasta, and breakfast cereals all come from plants.

16

We eat lots of different seeds called **grains**. Rice, wheat, oats, and barley are all grains.

◁ This is wheat grain. It is used to make bread.

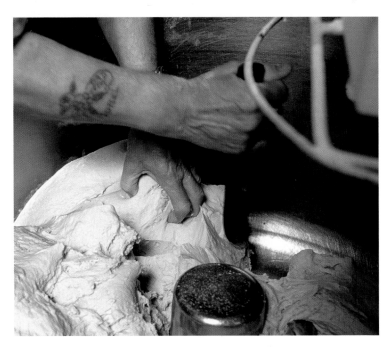

▲ Bread dough

Grain is ground into flour. This is mixed with water and **yeast** to make dough. The dough is baked into bread.

Next time you go shopping, look at different foods. Can you tell which come from plants?

Fruits and Vegetables

Fruits and vegetables come from different parts of a plant.

Fruits grow from the flowers of a plant. They have seeds inside them that will grow into new plants.

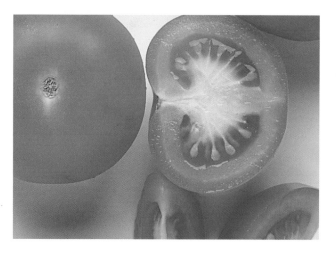

▲ These are all fruits, because they have seeds inside them. Even a tomato is a fruit.

We can eat other parts of a plant. They are called vegetables.

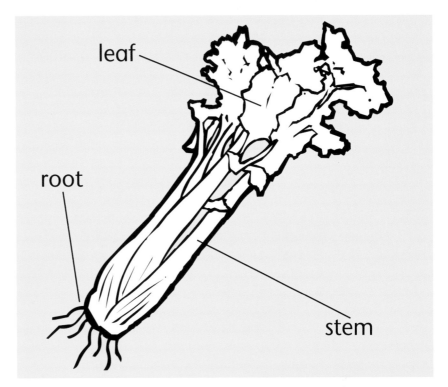

leaf

root

stem

▶ Celery plant

▲ We eat the leaves of a cabbage plant.

▲ We eat the **stem** of a celery plant.

▲ We eat the **root** of a carrot plant.

What other vegetables can you think of?
Are they the leaves, stems, or roots of a plant?

Poisonous Plants

Some plants can make us sick because they are **poisonous**.

▲ When we eat rhubarb, we eat the stem of the plant. Rhubarb leaves are poisonous to us.

▶ These are the flowers of a laburnum tree. Its flowers, seeds, leaves, and roots would all make us sick.

Mushrooms and toadstools
can be very poisonous.

Although mushrooms and toadstools
are not plants (they are called **fungi**),
they grow next to plants. You can find
them on lawns and in woods.

 When you touch plants or fungi, you
should always wash your hands
afterwards. You should never put
plants in your mouth unless you
know they are safe to eat.

Useful Plants

We use plants in many different ways. Cotton, rubber, and some medicines are made from plants.

◀ Cotton plants have green fruits that split open. Inside are seeds and white fibers.

▶ Cotton fibers are picked from the cotton plant. They are pulled out into long, thin threads and then woven into cloth.

Rubber comes from the liquid, or **sap**, inside a rubber tree.

◀ The liquid is called **latex**. It is used to make things such as car tires.

Plants are also used in medicines. Aspirin is made from the **bark** of a willow tree. Aspirin helps make us better when we have colds or headaches.

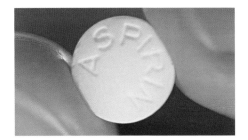

Many shampoos and soaps are made using plants such as coconut. Look at some labels and see what plants are in the ingredients.

Trees and Wood

Trees are plants. The trunk and branches of trees are made of wood. Wood is very useful.

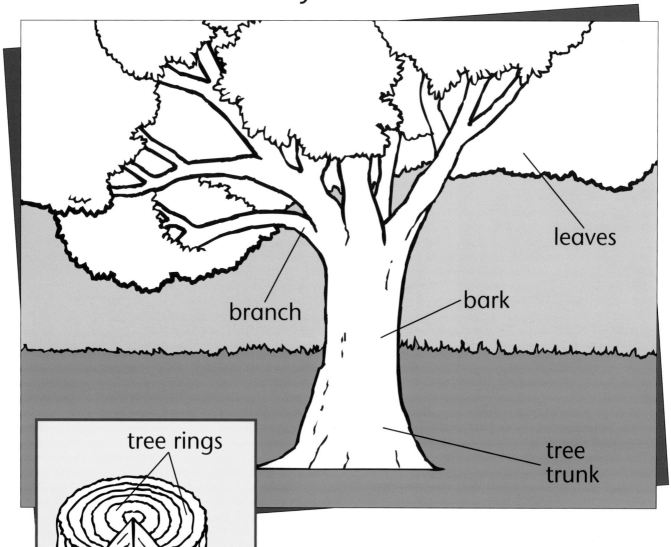

leaves

branch

bark

tree trunk

tree rings

wood

bark

◀ If you cut through a tree trunk and count the number of rings, you can tell the age of the tree. Each ring is one year of growth.

24

Wood is hard and can be cut into different shapes. It can be made into many things.

◀ This house is made of wood.

Look around your house. What can you find that is made of wood?

Looking after Plants

Plants are very useful. They provide food and shelter for people and animals. We need to look after plants.

▲ In our gardens and parks, we look after plants by making sure that they have enough light and water.

Rain forests are large tropical forests. They are hot and wet year-round.

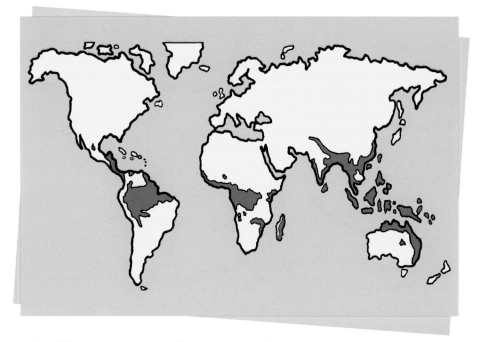

▲ This map shows where rain forests grow in the world.

Rain forests are home to many plants, birds, animals, and people. We need to look after their forest home and not chop too much of it down.

Amazing Plants

The longest seaweed, the Pacific giant kelp, can be almost 200 feet (60 m) long. It can grow about 18 inches (45 cm) in one day.

The biggest tree in the world is the Giant Sequoia. It can grow to be more than 260 feet (79 m) tall and be as wide as 80 feet (24 m). Sequoias are found in California.

The Douglas fir tree can grow to be more than 410 feet (125 m) tall. One of the tallest was found in British Columbia, Canada.

Use this book to find the answers to this Amazing Plants quiz!

- What kind of plant is a bamboo?

- Where are seeds made in most plants?

- On what type of trees can you find cones?

- Name two types of plants that have fronds instead of leaves.

- Where do plants make their food?

- What part of a cabbage plant do we eat?

- What part of a rhubarb plant is poisonous?

- How can you tell the age of a tree?

Glossary

bark   tough material that covers the outside of trees.

blossoms   flowers that grow on fruit trees.

chlorophyll   green coloring found in leaves and fronds.

cones   types of fruit that are found on conifer trees.

flower   part of a plant that is usually very colorful. The flower becomes the fruits and seeds of a flowering plant.

fronds   leaf-like part of some plants where spores grow.

fruits   parts of a plant that grow from the flower and protect the seed or seeds.

fungi   a group of living things (including mushrooms, toadstools, and yeast) that grow on other living things. One of the group on its own is called a fungus.

grains   cereal plants that are grown for food.

latex   milky liquid, or sap, that comes from the rubber tree.

leaves   parts of a plant that are usually green and use sunlight, air, and water to make food for the plant.

petals   outer parts of a flower that are often colorful.

poisonous   something that will make you sick if you eat or touch it.

rain forests   large, thick forests that grow in hot, damp places.

root   part of a plant that holds the plant in the soil. The roots take up water from the soil.

sap   milky liquid found inside plants.

seeds   small parts made in the flower of a flowering plant. When seeds are planted, new plants grow from them.

spores   seed-like parts that grow under the leaves of ferns and seaweed. New plants grow from spores.

stem   part of a plant that holds up the leaves and flowers. The stem carries water from the roots to the leaves.

vegetables   parts of a plant that are not the fruit, such as the flowers, stems, leaves, or roots.

yeast   type of fungus used to make bread.

Index